MAKING MONEY ONLINE: BOOK 10

By Michael Callum Mayaka

MAXIMIZING ONLINE INCOME OPPORTUNITIES

FOREWORD:

In today's digital age, making money online has become a viable and accessible option for individuals seeking financial independence or additional income streams. The internet offers a plethora of opportunities that allow you to leverage your skills, creativity, and resources to generate revenue. This guide aims to provide you with valuable insights, strategies, and practical tips on how to make money online effectively.

This book is part of a series for more information see Further reading at the end of this book.

Table of Contents

Foreword: 3

10. Maximizing Online Income Opportunities 5

    10.1 Diversifying Income Streams: The Key to Financial Stability and Growth 6

        There are several advantages to diversifying your income streams: 8

        Diversifying income streams can be achieved through various strategies, including: 11

    10.2 Building a Personal Brand 14

    10.3 Effective Marketing and Promotion 21

    10.4 Staying Motivated and Overcoming Challenges 29

Summary: 36

Further reading: 37

10. MAXIMIZING ONLINE INCOME OPPORTUNITIES

10.1 DIVERSIFYING INCOME STREAMS: THE KEY TO FINANCIAL STABILITY AND GROWTH

In an ever-changing and unpredictable economic landscape, relying on a single source of income can be risky. Diversifying your income streams is a strategy that can provide financial stability, security, and even the potential for growth. By creating multiple avenues through which money flows into your life, you can mitigate the risks associated with relying solely on one source and open up opportunities for increased income. Here, we will explore the concept of diversifying income streams and its benefits.

Diversifying income streams refers to the practice of generating income from multiple sources, often in different industries or sectors. This approach helps to distribute risk and ensures that if one income stream is affected by market fluctuations, economic downturns, or unexpected circumstances, you have other sources to rely on. By not putting all your eggs in one basket, you create a buffer against financial setbacks and enhance your overall financial resilience.

THERE ARE SEVERAL ADVANTAGES TO DIVERSIFYING YOUR INCOME STREAMS:

1. Increased Stability: Relying on a single income source leaves you vulnerable to unexpected disruptions. Diversification helps mitigate this risk by providing a safety net. If one income stream is temporarily or permanently affected, others can compensate for the loss, maintaining a level of financial stability.

2. Multiple Growth Opportunities: Diversification allows you to tap into various industries and sectors, providing

access to different growth potentials. If one income stream experiences limited growth or reaches saturation, you can explore new avenues that offer higher growth prospects, thereby expanding your overall earning potential.

3. Income Smoothing: Different income streams may have different earning patterns. Some may generate income consistently throughout the year, while others may have seasonal fluctuations. By diversifying, you can balance out these variances and create a more consistent cash flow, reducing financial stress and providing a steady income stream.

4. Adaptability and Flexibility: Diversification equips you with the ability to adapt to changing market conditions and economic trends. If one industry or sector faces challenges, you can pivot your focus to other income streams that are thriving, allowing you to capitalize on emerging opportunities.

5. Personal and Professional Development: Exploring different income streams often requires learning new skills, expanding your knowledge base, and embracing diverse experiences. This personal and professional growth can enhance your value in the marketplace, making you more versatile and adaptable.

DIVERSIFYING INCOME STREAMS CAN BE ACHIEVED THROUGH VARIOUS STRATEGIES, INCLUDING:

a) Creating passive income streams, such as investing in stocks, real estate, or dividend-paying assets.

b) Starting a side business or freelancing in addition to your primary job.

c) Monetizing your skills and expertise through consulting, coaching, or teaching online courses.

d) Generating income from digital assets, such as selling e-books, creating and licensing software, or selling stock photography.

It is important to note that diversification requires careful planning and research. Assess the risks, market conditions, and feasibility of each potential income stream before investing significant time and resources. Prioritize income streams that align with your interests, skills, and long-term goals, ensuring a sustainable and enjoyable income generation journey.

In conclusion, diversifying income streams is a smart financial strategy that reduces risk, enhances stability, and opens up new growth opportunities. By creating multiple sources of income, you build a more resilient financial foundation, increasing your chances of achieving long-term financial success and security. Embrace the mindset of diversification, adapt to changing circumstances, and continuously explore new income-generating avenues to safeguard your financial well-being.

10.2 BUILDING A PERSONAL BRAND

In today's digital age, building a personal brand has become increasingly important for individuals who want to stand out, establish credibility, and create new opportunities. A personal brand is the unique combination of your skills, expertise, values, and personality that distinguishes you from others in your field. It is how you present yourself to the world and how others perceive you. Whether you're an entrepreneur, freelancer, or professional seeking career advancement, building a strong personal brand can significantly impact your success. Here are some key considerations and strategies for building a personal brand:

1. Define Your Brand Identity: Start by defining your brand identity. Reflect on your strengths, passions, values, and unique qualities that set you apart. Consider your target audience and the specific niche or industry you want to be associated with. Develop a clear understanding of what you want your personal brand to represent.

2. Craft Your Brand Story: A compelling brand story helps others connect with you on a deeper level. Share your journey, experiences, and the challenges you've overcome. Be authentic and transparent in your storytelling. Communicate your mission, values, and what you can offer to your audience.

3. Consistency Across Platforms: Building a personal brand involves maintaining consistency across all your online and offline platforms. Ensure that your website, social media profiles, professional networks, and any other digital assets align with your brand identity. Use consistent visual elements, such as logos, colour schemes, and fonts, to create a cohesive brand experience.

4. Content Creation and Thought Leadership: Establishing yourself as a thought leader in your industry is crucial for building a personal brand. Create high-quality, relevant content that provides value to your audience. This can include blog posts, articles, videos, podcasts, or social

media updates. Share your expertise, insights, and opinions to position yourself as a trusted authority.

5. Engage and Network: Actively engage with your audience and build meaningful relationships with others in your industry. Respond to comments, participate in discussions, and offer support and advice. Attend industry events, conferences, and networking opportunities to connect with like-minded individuals. Collaborate with influencers or experts to expand your reach and credibility.

6. Online Reputation Management: Maintaining a positive online reputation is

essential for a strong personal brand. Regularly monitor your online presence and address any negative feedback or misinformation promptly and professionally. Engage in reputation management practices such as search engine optimization (SEO), monitoring social media mentions, and maintaining a consistent online presence.

7. Professional Development and Continuous Learning: To build a personal brand, it's important to continuously improve and expand your knowledge and skills. Stay updated with industry trends, attend webinars or workshops, and pursue certifications or advanced education. Position yourself as a lifelong learner and

someone who is dedicated to personal and professional growth.

8. Authenticity and Transparency: Building an authentic personal brand is crucial. Be true to yourself and your values. Avoid portraying an image that doesn't align with who you truly are. People appreciate genuine connections, so be open, transparent, and relatable in your interactions.

9. Seek Feedback and Adapt: Regularly seek feedback from your audience, peers, and mentors. Listen to constructive criticism and adapt accordingly. Stay open to evolving your personal brand as you grow personally and professionally.

Building a personal brand is an ongoing process that requires time, effort, and consistency. Stay true to your unique identity, provide value to your audience, and cultivate meaningful relationships. With perseverance and a well-crafted personal brand, you can enhance your professional opportunities, establish yourself as an authority, and create a lasting impact in your industry.

10.3 EFFECTIVE MARKETING AND PROMOTION

Marketing and promotion play a crucial role in the success of any online venture. In a highly competitive digital landscape, it is essential to stand out from the crowd and reach your target audience effectively. This article explores key strategies and techniques for effective marketing and promotion that can help you maximize your online success.

1. Define Your Target Audience: Understanding your target audience is the foundation of effective marketing. Identify their demographics, interests, and pain points. This knowledge will allow you to

tailor your marketing messages and select the most appropriate channels to reach them.

2. Develop a Strong Brand Identity: A compelling and consistent brand identity helps you differentiate yourself and build trust with your audience. Create a unique brand voice, visual elements, and messaging that resonate with your target market. This will help you establish a memorable presence in the online sphere.

3. Content Marketing: Producing valuable and engaging content is an effective way to attract and retain customers. Create content that addresses your audience's needs and

interests, such as blog posts, videos, infographics, and podcasts. Share your expertise, provide solutions, and establish yourself as an authority in your niche.

4. Search Engine Optimization (SEO): Optimizing your website and content for search engines is essential for organic visibility and traffic. Conduct keyword research to understand the terms and phrases your audience uses to find relevant content. Optimize your website structure, meta tags, headings, and content to improve your search engine rankings.

5. Social Media Marketing: Leverage the power of social media platforms to connect

with your audience and promote your products or services. Choose the platforms where your target audience is most active and create engaging content that encourages sharing and interaction. Utilize social media advertising to reach a wider audience and drive targeted traffic to your website.

6. Email Marketing: Building an email list allows you to nurture relationships with your audience and convert leads into customers. Offer valuable incentives, such as exclusive content or discounts, to encourage visitors to subscribe. Send regular, personalized emails that provide value and drive engagement.

7. Influencer Marketing: Collaborating with influencers in your industry can help expand your reach and build credibility. Identify influencers whose audience aligns with your target market and establish partnerships for content promotion or product endorsements. Ensure that the influencer's values and audience align with your brand to maximize the impact.

8. Pay-Per-Click (PPC) Advertising: PPC advertising, such as Google Ads or social media ads, allows you to target specific keywords or demographics and pay only when users click on your ads. Set clear goals, define your budget, and monitor your campaigns closely to optimize their

performance and maximize your return on investment (ROI).

9. Analyze and Optimize: Regularly monitor and analyze your marketing efforts to understand what works and what needs improvement. Utilize analytics tools to track website traffic, conversion rates, and user behaviour. Make data-driven decisions, test different strategies, and optimize your campaigns based on the insights gathered.

10. Build Relationships and Provide Excellent Customer Service: Focus on building strong relationships with your customers and providing exceptional customer service. Encourage feedback and

reviews, respond promptly to inquiries, and go above and beyond to exceed customer expectations. Satisfied customers become brand advocates and help spread positive word-of-mouth.

In conclusion, effective marketing and promotion are essential for online success. By defining your target audience, developing a strong brand identity, creating valuable content, optimizing for search engines, leveraging social media, utilizing email marketing, collaborating with influencers, utilizing PPC advertising, analyzing and optimizing campaigns, and building strong customer relationships, you can effectively promote your online venture, attract your target audience, and achieve your business goals. Stay proactive, adapt to changing trends, and continuously refine your marketing strategies to stay ahead in the dynamic digital landscape.

10.4 STAYING MOTIVATED AND OVERCOMING CHALLENGES

In any pursuit, whether it's making money online or achieving personal goals, staying motivated and overcoming challenges is crucial for success. The online world presents its own unique set of obstacles, but with the right mindset and strategies, you can navigate these challenges and stay motivated throughout your journey. Here are some key tips to help you in staying motivated and overcoming challenges:

1. Set Clear Goals: Clearly define your goals and break them down into smaller, actionable steps. This will give you a sense

of direction and make your objectives more manageable. Write them down and review them regularly to stay focused and motivated.

2. Visualize Success: Visualizing your desired outcome can be a powerful motivator. Create a vision board or regularly imagine yourself achieving your goals. This mental imagery can boost your motivation and keep you on track, especially during difficult times.

3. Find Your Purpose: Understand why you're pursuing your online endeavours. Identifying your purpose and aligning it with your goals will provide a strong

foundation for motivation. Remind yourself of the reasons why you started, and let them fuel your determination and resilience.

4. Break Down Challenges: Challenges are inevitable, but how you perceive and approach them makes a difference. Instead of viewing challenges as roadblocks, see them as opportunities for growth. Break them down into smaller, manageable tasks and tackle them one step at a time.

5. Seek Support and Accountability: Surround yourself with like-minded individuals who share similar goals or are on a similar journey. Join online communities, forums, or social media groups where you can connect with others who can provide

support, guidance, and accountability. Sharing your challenges and progress with others can motivate you to keep going.

6. Celebrate Milestones: Celebrate your achievements and milestones along the way. Recognize and reward yourself for reaching significant milestones, no matter how small they may seem. This positive reinforcement boosts motivation and keeps you engaged in the process.

7. Continuous Learning: Embrace a growth mindset and prioritize continuous learning. The online world is constantly evolving, and staying up-to-date with new trends, technologies, and strategies is crucial. Invest time in learning and acquiring new skills to

stay ahead of the curve and adapt to changes more effectively.

8. Take Breaks and Practice Self-Care: Burnout can hinder motivation and productivity. It's essential to take regular breaks, both short and extended, to recharge and rejuvenate. Practice self-care activities that help you relax, reduce stress, and maintain a healthy work-life balance. This will ultimately contribute to sustained motivation and overall well-being.

9. Stay Positive and Practice Gratitude: Maintain a positive attitude even during challenging times. Focus on the progress you've made and the lessons learned along

the way. Cultivate a habit of gratitude by expressing appreciation for the opportunities and successes you've achieved. This positive mindset will help you stay motivated and resilient in the face of challenges.

10. Learn from Setbacks: Setbacks are part of the journey. When faced with failure or setbacks, view them as valuable learning experiences. Analyze what went wrong, adjust your strategies if needed, and use these setbacks as stepping stones toward future success.

In conclusion, staying motivated and overcoming challenges is essential when making money online or pursuing any endeavour. By setting clear goals, visualizing success, seeking support, and maintaining a positive mindset, you can stay motivated and resilient throughout your online journey. Remember that challenges are opportunities for growth, and with determination, perseverance, and continuous learning, you can overcome obstacles and achieve your goals.

SUMMARY:

Making money online provides immense potential for individuals willing to explore the digital landscape. This guide has provided you with a comprehensive overview of various online income opportunities, ranging from e-commerce and freelancing to content creation and online tutoring. Remember, success in the online realm requires dedication, perseverance, and continuous learning. Stay proactive, adapt to changes, and embrace new opportunities to maximize your earning potential. With the right strategies and a positive mindset, you can turn your online endeavours into a rewarding and sustainable source of income.

FURTHER READING:

If you enjoyed this book, please consider reading one of the other books in the series:

Making Money Online: Book 1 (Understanding the Online Landscape)

Making Money Online: Book 2 (E-commerce and Online Retail)

Making Money Online: Book 3 (Freelancing and Remote Work)

Making Money Online: Book 4 (Content Creation and Monetization)

Making Money Online: Book 5 (Online Tutoring and Education)

Making Money Online: Book 6 (Online Surveys, Microtasks, and Rewards)

Making Money Online: Book 7 (Online Investments and Trading)

Making Money Online: Book 8 (Creating and Selling Digital Assets)

Making Money Online: Book 9 (Online Consulting and Coaching)

Making Money Online: Book 10 (Maximizing Online Income Opportunities)

All the books can be found on Amazon as Kindle and Paperback, or you can buy the complete edition which contains the full series in one book. The complete edition is available as Kindle, Paperback and exclusively as Hardback. You can find all the links in my book site: books.michaelmayaka.co.uk.

www.ingramcontent.com/pod-product-compliance
Lightning Source LLC
Chambersburg PA
CBHW041943240526
45473CB00033B/498